To Reach a Reason

Finding Spiritual Fulfillment as a Caregiver

D. Rogers

WestBow Press books may be ordered through booksellers or by contacting:

WestBow Press
A Division of Thomas Nelson & Zondervan
1663 Liberty Drive
Bloomington, IN 47403
www.westbowpress.com
1 (866) 928-1240

Scripture quotations taken from the New American Standard Bible®, Copyright © 1960, 1962, 1963, 1968,
1971, 1972, 1973, 1975, 1977, 1995 by The Lockman Foundation. Used by permission." (www.Lockman.org)

ISBN: 978-1-5127-0629-1 (sc)
ISBN: 978-1-5127-0630-7 (e)

Print information available on the last page.

WestBow Press rev. date: 09/14/2015

WESTBOW
PRESS®
A DIVISION OF THOMAS NELSON
& ZONDERVAN

Contents

Introduction

To Reach a Reason

*T*his is the *true story* of the way **God** unfolded his will and his word as he showed me how to reach a reason through wisdom, strength, and hope as a caregiver. **My mom's affliction with Alzheimer's disease became a journey into how God can turn a life for those affected into blessings beyond measure.**

I believe that my faith has unfolded a consciousness within my spirit that allowed me to reach a reason for this journey. I believe God directed me, as the progression of my mom's illness began to saturate her life, to focus on the continued significance of her life. She could still be a help and a hope to other people. For example, having found out about a study for Alzheimer's patients, my mom was able to participate (during the early stage of her illness) in a medical study with other participants all over the country to help others learn more about the disease. The Alzheimer's Disease Cooperative Study, University of California, San Diego, allowed my mom to participate and help with the design of future studies of potential Alzheimer's treatments. The local staff in Cleveland, Ohio, administered and managed the DHA clinical trial, which lasted for more than a year. They would share the study with the scientific community, and her contribution would have a lasting effect.

Also, my mom continued to attend and participate in various activities at a senior center and in adult day programs. She tried to help and assist others during her attendance at the senior center. People were blessed by her friendship and quiet spirit. Many of the seniors she met looked out for her and provided assistance when she was in need. Their kindness and compassion were gifts they freely shared with her. The staff also said that my mom's smile was a blessing to them.

My mom could still go for short walks outdoors, walks in the mall, attend outdoor events (such as musical concerts), participate in family gatherings, take short trips to visit family, and attend Saturday mass. Though my mom's Alzheimer's disease had an effect on her human connection with the world, amazingly, her spiritual connection continued to maintain its own existence. The rosary, for example, remained an important focus in her mind regarding her Christianity. Early in her illness, she sought to pray daily with her rosary, and while able to attend mass, she could recite specific prayers without any interruptive distraction. It was as if her spiritual being was one of two persons, although her human presence was slipping away.

After a period of time, my mom was eventually confined to home. She had a sense of peacefulness with the presence of family around her. God's purpose was to direct my mom's life down a path that our family did not expect, but at the same time, his purpose and plan directed our family toward the completion of his will through her illness. Our goal as a family was to care for her needs. This was a challenging venture, but it was also a blessing to have her at home. With God's intervention, worry turned into wisdom, struggle turned into strength, and hardship turned into hope.

Chapter 1

A Reason for This Spiritual Journey

D. Rogers

*I*reflect on the late 1970s when I made the decision to pursue the field of gerontology, the study of aging. During a routine visit, my mom's medical doctor inquired about my area of interest in college. When she told him gerontology, he said, "What is that?"

Alzheimer's disease—an illness that afflicts the brain, thus causing a large number of nerve cells in the brain to die[1]—was a part of my studies in attaining my degree. However, nothing could have prepared me, thirty years later, for the paralyzing dose of reality given to my siblings and me when our mom's doctor told us that Mom, being only in her mid-sixties, had Alzheimer's disease. I always thought she would be like the vibrant and energetic seniors (in their seventies, eighties, and beyond) who lived fruitful and fulfilling lives. We were about to walk through a door and toward a journey for which there would be no return.

My mom's symptoms, from mild and moderate to severe,[2] gradually progressed for ten years. Our family wanted her to have the best possible care, and we maintained as much as possible to allow her a sense of daily normality. This in itself was a gift from God. We will never fully understand why this illness became a part of her life, but we decided to accept this as God's will, despite the unfolding uncertainty of it all. Why she was given this illness to endure for the remainder of her life, only God knew.

---

1   Bibliography
"Caring for a Person with Alzheimer's Disease: Your Easy-to-Use Guide," National Institute on Aging. www.nia.nih.gov/Alzheimers. Last accessed March 2012.

2   Bibliography
"Caring for a Person with Alzheimer's Disease: Your Easy –to-Use Guide," National Institute on Aging. www.nia.nih.gov/Alzheimers. Last accessed March 2012.

I realize that we will never fully understand why situations happen as they do, but we can try, through God's love and understanding to reach a reason. In turn, we use that reason for spiritual growth and awareness to enlighten and strengthen others who are traveling a similar road. During this spiritual journey, I found an abundance of daily *wisdom, strength,* and *hope* within several passages of scripture in the Bible. These passages kept me going during the darkest and most challenging times. I want to share these most significant and poignant readings with the hope that they will be a blessing to those who are traveling this journey. In these passages, may others find comfort and peace. If you have already taken this journey, I pray you can take away something that will permeate the direction of God's will for your life.

Chapter 2

Wisdom

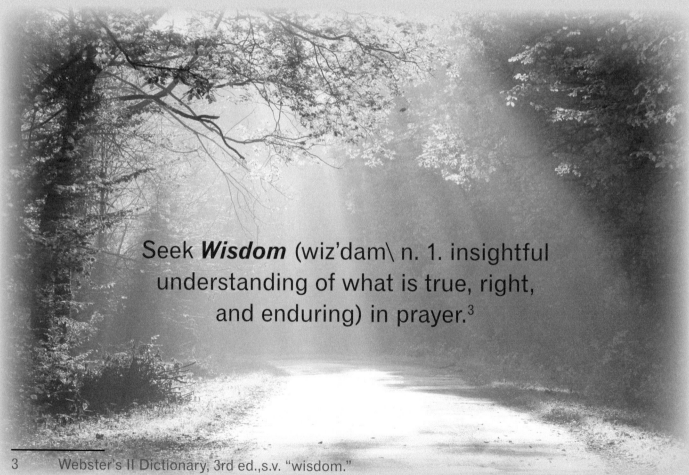

Seek **Wisdom** (wiz'dam\ n. 1. insightful understanding of what is true, right, and enduring) in prayer.[3]

---

3   Webster's II Dictionary, 3rd ed.,s.v. "wisdom."

When faced with the unexpected challenge of caring for a loved one with Alzheimer's disease, seeking medical interventions is usually the first step. But do you also turn to the Bible for answers as well? A caregiver desires to understand why this role is a part of their God's life journey. This journey may only be for a short time, or it may take several years. In either case, turning to the Bible for answers summons a sense of awareness that allows wisdom to become second nature. It will take time to absorb this concept (if it has never been explored), but seeking God in the presence of surrendering humbleness will open the door for God's wisdom and guidance. Remember and believe!

In the Bible, 1 Corinthians 10:13 says, "No test has been sent you that does not come to all men."

Besides, God keeps his promise. He will not let you be tested beyond your strength. Along with the test, he will give you a way out of it so that you may be able to endure it. People are more familiar with the paraphrase of this verse: "He will not put more on you than you can bear."

Many have heard these words before, but in reality, attempting to live without the strength of this verse only generates a sense of uncertainty in God's confidence in us. I realized this challenging journey was interwoven within where God wanted me to be, and who he wanted me to be regarding his purpose and plan.

Proverbs 3:5–6 in the Bible says, "Trust in the Lord with all your heart, on your own intelligence rely not; in all your ways be mindful of him, and he will make straight your paths."

Weeks had passed when I realized that the initial medical personnel and support our family sought was not as susceptive to our needs as we had hoped, so I prayed for wisdom and direction for the next step. Approximately a month later, I received a phone call at work from a senior who wanted to seek options regarding her eligibility for benefits and services.

She was a very engaging person who spoke about herself, her family, and the need for assistance. She also spoke about experiencing episodes of memory loss and her concern about the situation. She said her daughter relied on her for babysitting, getting the grandchildren from school, and other chores. She said she also expressed her memory loss concern to her doctor, and he directed her to medical services in the area of geriatrics. She provided me details of what became a positive outcome. As a result, she received help to improve her daily cognitive function.

During our conversation, I talked to the woman about my mom's diagnosis of an early onset of Alzheimer's disease. I explained to her how our family wanted to find better medical interventions and support. The woman provided me with medical information so I could pursue this new avenue for my mom. The process entailed monthly medical appointments across town to get the help my mom needed. The distance I had to travel was inconsequential because my mom and our family received so much support and care. My mom's condition reached a stable plateau for a number of years. I felt so blessed because the woman who sought assistance through our office could have gone to another co-worker. In seeking God's wisdom, she served as a sought-after blessing and the reason to an answered prayer.

Proverbs 3:13–15

Happy the man who finds wisdom, the man who gains understanding! For her profit is better than profit in silver, and better than gold is her revenue; she is more precious than corals, and none of your choice possessions can compare to her.

Chapter 3

Strength

Seek **Strength** (strengkth, strength, strength\ n. 1. the quality, state or property of being strong: power) in prayer.[4]

---

4   Webster's II Dictionary, 3rd ed.,s.v. "strength."

*F*rom a caregiver's point of view, each day is an attachment to the responsibilities of a loved one with Alzheimer's disease. Taking care of a loved one requires a flexible perspective of both strength and prayer. Surprisingly, many people do not always equate the two. However, in reality, they are both infused in mind and spirit.

We must not only rely on our own strength, but also on God's strength for direction and guidance, because we do not know what is around the corner of our loved one's illness. Many things are unpredictable, and Alzheimer's disease affects every person differently. My family and I were fortunate to have had the support of people who helped care for my mom when she attended a local senior center and adult day care centers during the duration of her illness. She participated for as long as she was able in these programs. It was a daily responsibility to provide for the needs of my mom. Some days were more challenging than others were. Upon arriving home each night, it was a priority for me to pray and thank God for the strength and blessings of another day.

In our spirit, we must strive to find strength in prayer from God. One night, after coming home from caring for my mom, I began to pray in spite of my complete exhaustion. God directed me through the power of the Holy Spirit to several of the most passionate passages of scripture, which allowed me to understand just how close God wanted me to be to him.

The first scripture came from Philippians 4:13: "In him who is the source of my strength, I have strength for everything."

The second scripture came from Philippians 4:19: "My God in turn will supply your needs fully, in a way worthy of his magnificent riches in Christ Jesus."

This find astonished me. It was as if I had found a treasure in an uninhabited territory. An overwhelming sense of peace permeated my spirit, and I realized that as long as I stayed on my knees in prayer, I would be given the strength to accomplish everything I needed for this journey.

Make prayer the most important step you take in order for God to give you a guiding hand of strength in your role as a caregiver. As you pray daily for strength in mind and in spirit, each day will become a reason for celebration of what God has been able to help you accomplish for both yourself and your loved one.

Chapter 4

Hope

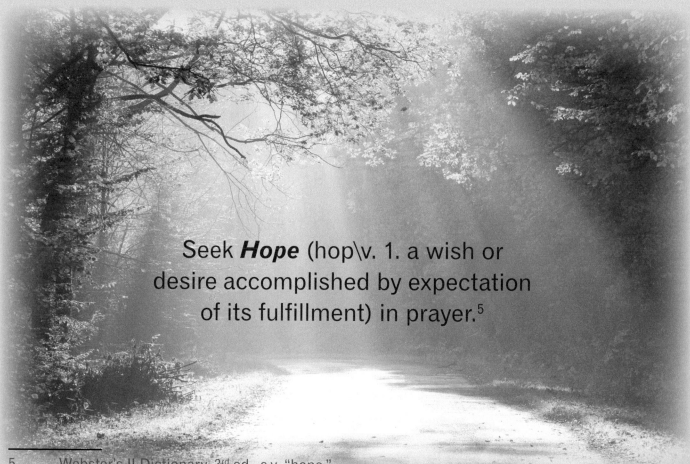

Seek **Hope** (hop\v. 1. a wish or
desire accomplished by expectation
of its fulfillment) in prayer.[5]

---

5   Webster's II Dictionary, 3rd ed., s.v. "hope."

*I*n spite of the growing challenges that my family and I faced as caregivers, we wanted to remain hopeful that our mom would remain at home until she passed away. During the earlier years of her illness, my mom regularly attended church, and she still had the ability to recite the prayers of her religious upbringing. As her Alzheimer's disease progressed, and she had reached the middle stage of the disease, it became progressively difficult for her to participate in this focal part of her life.

My sister asked me to care for Mom while she attended weekly Sunday church services with her family. I fell into a comfortable routine with my mom. My sister and I would meet again within the hour, and then later in the morning, I attended church with my own family. During my mom's time with me, she and I returned to my home, and on other occasions, we took car rides to enjoy the scenery of the seasons.

As weeks passed, thoughts grew in my spirit that I had something to do. I had to communicate my feelings and thoughts to my mom, and God's encouragement helped me to accomplish this task. My desire to express myself in a loving and compassionate way was foremost in my mind. I wanted my mom to know that time gave me a unique perspective. I wanted her to know that I appreciated her love and devotion to the family, even though it meant making difficult decisions on our behalf. When you are a child, your mind's limited understanding can only go so far, as you take everything at face value.

Now with my own family, I can stretch my understanding beyond this initial perspective. Some people may not be able to reach an understanding of how God's work, through the power of the Holy Spirit, connects all of our experiences in life for the greater good.

Sunday was here, and I knew this was the day to talk with my mom. I met my sister and picked up Mom. I drove for a short time while my mom was in the backseat viewing the pages of a magazine. Her illness had begun to limit her verbal communication. She was not able to make complete sentences, and I was not sure just how much she was able to comprehend. However, I was willing to be simplistic in my approach and allow God to give me the right words.

I said, "Ma, I have wanted to tell you how much I have appreciated all of the good things you have done for me, though I have not always expressed this through my actions. I've allowed myself to forgive you when I thought you were not always the perfect parent."

As I spoke, I tried to keep eye contact with my mom. In turn, she kept her eyes intent on me as if she were connecting a life force to every word.

I continued, "But most importantly, I ask for your forgiveness for me not expressing enough appreciation to you for the way God has helped you do all that you did for our family. I know that it was not easy."

There was a long pause. My mom did not say anything. In my thoughts, I was not even sure she would be able to respond due to the progressiveness of her Alzheimer's disease. Then I said, "Is it okay for us?"

Suddenly she said, "I hope so."

I was so shocked, yet at the same time amazed and thankful for her response. In my heart, I knew that God had given us this moment as a gift, which would remain with me for the rest of my life.

An important element for reflection, regarding an approach to any situation as a caregiver, is hope. God gives us this intangible gift despite our missteps and regrets. Hope pushes us forward, even when we take a few steps backward. If you are faced with a situation regarding how to reach a middle ground, search for Luke 12:12 in the Bible where Jesus said, "The Holy Spirit will teach you at that moment all that should be said."

My family and I look back at everything we were able to accomplish in the care of our mom, and we are so thankful to God for a prayer answered, as he allowed her to remain at home until she passed away. This was only due to the determinate wisdom, strength, and hope he gave us each day.

Chapter 5

A Caregiver's Reason for Prayer

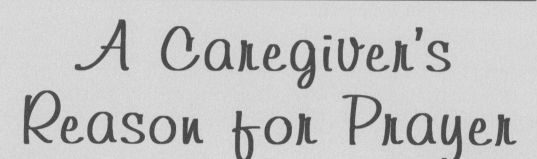

$\mathcal{E}$ach stage of Alzheimer's disease (mild, moderate, and severe) [6]carries its own unique challenges. As a caregiver, strive to reach a reason to have wisdom, strength, and hope as each stage of this illness progresses. As this progression takes its inevitable place, prayer will become an increasing mainstay and an anchoring foundation. An unwavering trust in God becomes crucial to sustaining your faith during the most challenging situations.

The Bible notes the following passage in 1 John 5:14–15: "We have this confidence in God; that he hears us whenever we ask for anything according to his will. And since we know that he hears us whenever we ask, we know that what we have asked him for is ours."

Readings in the Bible reinforce the pursuit of wisdom, strength, and hope during your role as a caregiver. You can find the following passages throughout the Bible, and I encourage you to immerse yourself in these readings in order to make the connection with God in your daily life.

Wisdom

Wisdom is one of those intangible gifts that we receive from God through the power of the Holy Spirit. It is a presence all its own and can direct us in our lives to face life's challenges. A caregiver who is caring for a loved one with Alzheimer's should seek and embrace God's wisdom. There will be times when decisions must be made, and who but God, the person who has nothing but the best in store for those who seek him, can help accomplish this task? Pray daily for wisdom. It is the best way to begin and end the day. Reign in your thoughts to accept situations as they come, and pray to God with an expressed appreciation for just how much he

---

6   Bibliography
"Caring for a Person with Alzheimer's Disease: Your Easy –to-Use Guide," National Institute on Aging. www.nia.nih.gov/Alzheimers. Last accessed March 2012.

has given you. Also, be thankful for what you have been able to accomplish on a daily basis. For example, instead of complaining that you have to wash clothes and linens daily for your loved one, instead say, "Thank you, God, for my good washing machine, which helps me take care of these items for my loved one." For the two steps you take backward, say thank you, God, for the one step you take forward.

Deuteronomy 4:29–30

Yet there too you shall seek the Lord, your God, and you shall indeed find him when you search after him with your whole heart and your whole soul.

In the care of my mom, I wanted to seek the Lord in order to understand what he wanted me to accomplish according to his will. I immersed my thoughts into prayer for direction and guidance.

In your distress, when all these things shall have come upon you, you shall finally return to the Lord, your God, and heed his voice.

Taking on a burden alone is an insurmountable battle. In taking his hand to seek guidance, God is with you for the duration.

Psalms 32:8

I will instruct you and show you the way you should walk, I will counsel you, keeping my eye on you.

The Lord is amazing in his way. He will work with you. Through the power of the Holy Spirit, he will guide each of your steps to care for you and your loved one.

Psalms 34:5

I sought the Lord, and he answered me and delivered me from all my fears.

The Lord will help you with your uncertainties and fears if you seek him in faith about the future.

Psalms 37:3

Commit to the Lord your way; trust him, and he will act.

Stay committed to yourself and your relationship with the Lord. Trust him to guide you with his still, small voice.

Psalms 38:16

Because of you, O Lord, I wait: you O Lord my God, will answer.

Sometimes we have to wait for answers to truths we do not understand. Patience and a willing conscience to listen to what God has to say will bring a peaceful and directive confidence.

Psalms 145:18

The Lord is near to all who call upon him, to all who call upon him in truth.

Always remember that the truth will set you free to love God with an open heart.

Hebrews 13:5

God has said, "I will never desert you, nor will I forsake you."

Sometimes in times of distress, we want to forsake ourselves. The God who loves us will never be far from our prayers.

Daniel 2:21

He gives wisdom to the wise and knowledge to those who understand.

Wisdom can direct caregivers to the opportunities, which allow us to do everything we need to do for our loved one with Alzheimer's disease.

Strength

Strive through prayer to reach a reason to have strength as a caregiver. Strength will help you develop a strong will to do what has to be done for your loved one with Alzheimer's disease. Many people work full time or part time and rely on outside resources for assistance. Other caregivers are at home with the full responsibility for care. In either scenario, getting on your knees to pray to God for strength will carry you beyond yourself. At the end of each day, I found comfort in reading Philippians 4:13 that says, "In him who is the source of my strength, I have strength for everything."

Additional passages from the Bible will also give strength to a caregiver:

Galatians 6:2

Help carry one another's burdens; in that way you will fulfill the law of Christ.

Even as you care for a loved one with Alzheimer's disease, helping someone else with an encouraging word and a prayer who is facing the same challenge can make you feel good.

2 Corinthians 12:8–10

Three times, I begged the Lord that this might leave me. He said to me, "My grace is enough for you, for in weakness power reaches perfection." And so I willingly boast of my weakness instead, that the power of Christ may rest upon me.

Therefore, I am content with weakness, with mistreatment, with distress, with persecutions and difficulties for the sake of Christ; for when I am powerless, it is then that I am strong.

Affirm within yourself that you will not bring your doubts and fears to fruition. They are unassuming intruders that can dilute your faith.

In prayer, it is all right to admit to the Lord that you are not perfect, as doubt promotes a salient perspective that you cannot always do it all. Seek a prayer partner who can keep you positive and uplifted in the Lord.

Hebrews 13:16

Thus, we may say with confidence, "The Lord is my helper, I will not be afraid; what can man do to me?"

Do not be afraid to ask the Lord for help. He is just waiting for you to ask him.

Psalms 37:23–24

By the Lord are the steps of a man made firm, and he approves his way. Though he falls, he does not lie prostrate, for the hand of the Lord sustains him.

Admit to yourself in prayer that for every two steps you take, you may take three steps backward. It will still be okay.

2 Timothy 1:7

The spirit God has given us is not a cowardly spirit, but rather one that makes us strong, loving, and wise.

God wants you to draw from him strength, love, and wisdom. Just ask and you shall receive. Believe, for in his time, and in his will, you will receive those beautiful and intangible gifts.

Psalms 138:3

When I called, you answered me; you built up strength within me.

God's strength will help you get through the tough times.

Isaiah 40:31

They that hope in the Lord will renew their strength, they will soar as with eagles' wings; they will run and not grow weary, walk and not grow faint.

Just keep going down the path of the Lord's will and look neither right nor left. Your strength will be renewed daily.

Mathew 11:28–30

Come to me, all you who are weary and find life burdensome, and I will refresh you. Take my yoke upon your shoulders and learn from me, for I am gentle and humble of heart. Your souls will find rest, for my yoke is easy and my burdens light.

Walk with Jesus, and he will walk with you to endure. He will reveal the walk for you with his guiding hand. Claim his words so they may carry you in his arms of protection. Let him lift you through your challenges.

Hope

Sometimes trial and error brings about the best solutions for a caregiver. The point is to maintain a positive perspective and approach to each challenge as it unfolds. Pray daily to reach a reason to have hope. It is that hope in God's plan that will help you care for your loved one with Alzheimer's disease. Hope will allow him to reveal everything to you in his time and in his own way for the greater good of all.

Lamentations 3:25–26

Good is the Lord to one who waits for him to the soul that seeks him, it is good to hope in silence for the saving help of the Lord.

It is important to know that your life for a certain point in time is not hopeless. Direction comes from the Lord who is the source of all hope. Have hope in your abilities with the Lord as your guide.

Psalms 145:14

The Lord lifts up all who are falling and raises up all who are bowed down.

The Lord wants you to maintain a mature perspective and know that you will not always accomplish every task. He will carry you and care for you if you let Him.

Psalms 145:18

The Lord is near to all who call upon him, to all who call upon him in truth.

Your journey is not isolated. Pray to the Lord and ask him to walk with you. He is waiting to hear from you. In truth, give him everything, the good, and the bad, and then leave the rest to him.

D. Rogers

1 Corinthians 13:13

There are in the end three things that last: faith, hope, and love, and the greatest of these is love.

Have faith in God's ability to help you accomplish your role as a caregiver. The Lord will generate the love you need as a caregiver, both for yourself and for your loved one.

Romans 15:13

So may God, the source of hope, fill you with all joy and peace in believing so that through the power of the Holy Spirit you may have hope in abundance.

With God's help and through the power of the Holy Spirit, allow wisdom, strength, and hope to enter into your life so that your faith can mature each day. Your loved one with Alzheimer's needs you. In whatever capacity you can provide, always remember that God's abundance is a promise. He will always provide hope for you and your loved one.

Chapter 6

A Reason to Have Faith

At my mom's routine medical appointment, the doctor noted some progressive symptoms in her illness. The doctor then gave me the grave and unexpected news—Mom had approximately two weeks to live. It was hard to comprehend the words. It was as if he spoke to me in a foreign language, and I had the doctor repeat the inexplicable news. I will never forget his sincerely compassionate manner. I left the doctor's office with my mom, and then I quietly broke down in tears. She was unable to comprehend my anguished helplessness. I asked God to give me strength to endure the turbulence of my emotions. Upon our arrival home, I broke the news to my sister and other siblings. Hospice services were called, and we allowed our minds to focus on Mom's care.

Two weeks had almost passed when the progressive decline of my mom's health become more apparent. Her breathing had become progressively labored, she had been non-verbal, and her eyes had remained closed for most of the two-week period. During the later part of the two weeks, my siblings and I kept an evening vigil around her.

All of the family remained close, made her comfortable, and talked to her. Late into the second night of the two-week period, my sister noticed that Mom's eyes had opened. She was looking wide-eyed up toward her bedroom ceiling as if looking at something above. Slowly, her labored breathing began to fade. It was during the middle of the night, and our quiet surroundings began to blend in with the faint stillness of her breathing. Everyone in the house began to surround her, as we realized she was leaving us. I believe she knew it was time; she had to leave us behind.

Then we saw a tear roll down her face from her left eye. My sister gently wiped her tear away and closed her eyes. All of the family surrounded my mom and began to pray. I lay down next to my mom and began touching her face, still feeling the warmth of her skin. I wanted to feel the warmth as long as I could, as if she was still with us. Slowly, that warmth began to fade. It was only then that I felt like my mom had crossed over with the angels and into God's hands. My mom went with God on March 8, 2011, at 3:40 a.m. This was not the end of her life, but a continuation of her life through her family.

We illustrated a beautiful narration of her life at the funeral. Family members from around the world and her lifelong friends acknowledged and admired her.

Several months later, now having our mom laid to rest with our dad, it was almost Christmas. I placed a Christmas wreath on my mom's newly engraved headstone. I allowed myself to become absorbed with the peacefulness of my surroundings. The day was gray and filled with mist from the moisture in the air. The mixture of wet snow and rain contributed to the almost still, mystic setting. I could not ignore the conflict within me of both peacefulness and sadness, knowing that this was an inevitable chapter in my life.

I reflected to a year ago, to the exact day, March 14, 2010. It was my brother-in-law's birthday. My sister planned a party for him. We celebrated and played calypso music. Everyone in the family enjoyed themselves. I felt the urge to dance with my mom so she could enjoy the party with us. I guided her with both hands, and she was able to follow my lead for a brief time. At this phase of her illness, her verbal communication was virtually nonexistent. As the music ended, everyone gave applause for her accomplishment. It was a wonderful memory.

March 14, 2011 served to be the day we would all gather as a family to say our final good-byes. As I ended these thoughts, I directed my thoughts to prayer. As I proceeded to my car, I could not help but notice how the sun began to slowly slide through a curtain of clouds that opened up the sky. The rays descended to the ground and onto the gravestone, which created a luminous affect. As I looked up at the sky, it seemed as though the sun's rays reflected onto the gravestone. I could not help but think that God was trying to remind me to have faith in his infinite love and presence in which we all try to understand.

My parents – Mr. and Mrs. Whitson

Chapter 7

A Caregiver's Reason to Reach Others

A staff member at a hospital made a presentation request: to help provide resources and benefit information for geriatric patients and their caregivers. Often times I fulfill such a request as part of my workday schedule. As I sat in the office waiting to be announced, I saw a young woman at a distance, also in the waiting area. She was told that a doctor would see her in a few minutes. Her expression of exhaustion was evident as she yawned and said, "I am so tired."

I turned in the direction of the young woman and she continued, "My mom's dementia keeps me from getting enough rest at night. I have food all over my clothes because my mom threw her breakfast at me, and I did not have time to change my clothes. All I wanted to do was make it to this appointment on time. I know I look terrible."

I asked her, "Has your mom been diagnosed with Alzheimer's disease?"

"Yes."

The young woman continued to explain her mother's symptoms. She said she had turned down respite care because she felt it was her responsibility to care for her mom. Now that her mom's symptoms had progressed, the increasing demands had begun to take a toll on her, and she was seeking answers and help.

I was eager to provide her information, having explained that my mom had Alzheimer's disease for ten years. I explained how my family and I were able to care for her at home until her passing. By this time, it had been fourteen months since my mom had passed away.

As we talked, the young woman continued to apologize through her expressive yawns of exhaustion, which continued to permeate our conversation. She thanked me for the resources and information I gave her to share with her family.

An expressive display of euphoric enthusiasm came pouring out of me. I was so happy to help a perfect stranger; we were in a sorority of sorts, which predestined us to become members.

Then I said, "Turning to the Lord in prayer for wisdom, strength, and hope will take you to a place to help get you through the most challenging of times."

Our conversation meshed into an awakening of words. Both of us reached a sort of a passing of a torch, which I once carried and now I was giving to her.

Our conversation was suddenly cut short by the announcement of her appointment with the doctor. The young woman thanked me for the assistance.

Upon my leaving the office, the nurse who escorted me to the exit apologized for the busy morning of patients, which delayed the time of my presentation.

"It was not a problem," I said. "It gave me an opportunity to talk to a caregiver in the waiting area while a doctor was seeing her mom. I gave her some information and resources for her and her family, and I shared the experience of my family also being caregivers of a parent with Alzheimer's disease."

"See, there was a reason why you were here," said the nurse. "This was where God wanted you to be."

Both surprised and fulfilled by her response, I said, "Absolutely!"

Several months later, while reading my Bible, I discovered the following affirmation of my reason as a caregiver, to reach others.

2 Corinthians 1:3--4

Praised be God, the Father of our Lord Jesus Christ,

the Father of mercies, and the God of all consolation!

He comforts us in all our afflictions and thus enables us

to comfort those who are in trouble with the same consolation

we have received from him.

God never ceases to amaze when it comes to the abundance of his blessings!

Final Words of Prayer

Whether you are caring for a loved one with Alzheimer's at home or are assuring the resident is cared for in a nursing facility, believe that God will provide everything you will need for your loved one. As I have mentioned before, your most powerful tools are prayer and a Bible. It is with a most sincere heart that I leave you with a gift of prayer.

I will be praying this prayer for you and with you daily.

Many blessings.

Dear God,

In prayer, I beseech you to hold the caregivers of a loved one with Alzheimer's near, to take away their uncertainty, to take away their fear.

Just when they think they cannot carry on, hold them a little closer, God, so they may receive your inner peace and calm.

When they cease to understand the direction of your guiding hand, open their hearts to embrace your words and seek your divine plan.

Amen.

Bookmark

Acknowledgments

For my parents, who were married for approximately thirty-five years. Their examples of hard work and commitment to family illustrated what was most important to them. This was their legacy and greatest gift to the family.

For my youngest sister, Arlana, who found immeasurable strength and courage to care for my mom around the clock during the most challenging times of her illness.

For Celeste, my sister in Detroit, who cared for my mom during the holidays and did not hesitate to do as much as she could for her care.

For my brother, Deland, who helped us keep a vigil with the family as my mom gave us time to say our good-byes.

For my brothers-in-law, George and Kevin, the greatest guys, who have complemented our family. During the care of my mom, they did not hesitate to help when called upon.

To my husband, Kenneth, who was always there to provide immeasurable love and support.

For my nieces, Ariana, Allysa, Ariel, Alexis, and Jasmine, as well as my nephew, Justin who grew to understand my mom's illness. They faced challenges, but their compassion for their grandma was a true blessing.

For my son, Kenneth Jr., and my daughter, Chelsea, who pitched in to help their grandma.

For my cousin Juanita for her support, wisdom, and prayers.

For Ms. Smith, my mom's best friend, many thanks for being there for our family; and to Celia for her prayers.

For our family in Trinidad, West Indies, who constantly prayed for us.

To Ms. Dickson, who kept our family in prayer and provided words of encouragement.

To my sisters in Christ (Gwen, Grenee, and Clara), the chosen women of God who came to visit with my mom and provided the ministry of song and worship.

To all of our many friends and longtime neighbors who provided so much encouragement and support to our family.

Following are the dedicated and skilled people who provided their God-given skills and compassion throughout the years regarding the medical care for my mom and support for our family:

Hoon Park, MD, and staff, University Hospitals Medical Practices

Babak Tousi, MD, FACP, and staff, Cleveland Clinic/Lakewood Hospital Senior Care Assessment Center

John J. Sanitato Jr., MD, Lutheran Hospital

The staff of Ernest J. Bohn Golden Age Center

Alzheimer's Association, Cleveland Area Chapter

Gateway Family House, Adult Day Program

The staff of the Eliza Bryant Adult Day Program

The staff of the Uh Foley Elderhealth Center at Fairhill Center/DHA study

About the Author

D. Rogers has worked in the field of aging with various organizations for thirty years.

She was born in Cleveland, Ohio. She has a bachelor of science in gerontology, a masters in non-profit organizations, and she completed the American Society on Aging New Ventures in Leadership (NVL) program as a NVL research partner.

She lives in Cleveland, Ohio, with her husband and two children.

She is first lady of her church and serves with her husband, who is pastor of the church.

This is her first book.

Notes

Printed in the United States
by Baker & Taylor Publisher Services